Original title:
Embers of Connection

Author: Daisy Dewi
ISBN HARDBACK: 978-1-80560-271-2
ISBN PAPERBACK: 978-1-80560-736-6

A Bond Beyond

In whispers shared beneath the stars,
Two souls unite, no distance far.
Through storms and sun, they stand as one,
A bond unbroken, never done.

With laughter ringing in the air,
They weave a tale beyond compare.
For every tear and joyful cheer,
Together they'll conquer every fear.

The Hearth of Friendship

At the hearth where warmth resides,
Friendship blooms, no need to hide.
In gentle talks by the firelight,
Hearts entwined, spirits bright.

With shared stories and secret dreams,
Life feels richer than it seems.
Through thick and thin, they stand by each,
A living bond no words can teach.

Traces of Light

In shadows deep, a spark ignites,
A trace of hope, a guiding light.
Through darkest days, they find a way,
Together shining, come what may.

With every laugh, each tear they share,
They weave a glow that fills the air.
In quiet moments, friendships grow,
A light that dances, soft and low.

Interwoven Hearts

Two hearts entwined like threads of gold,
In the tapestry of life, stories told.
Through trials faced and laughter shared,
In every moment, love declared.

Their bond, a weave of joy and pain,
In every heartache, love will reign.
Together breathing, pulse and beat,
A song of friendship, bittersweet.

Bonds Ignited in Twilight

In the fading light, whispers bloom,
Two hearts entwined, dispelling gloom.
A gentle touch, a knowing glance,
In twilight's hold, we find our dance.

Stars awaken, casting dreams,
Amongst the shadows, love redeems.
With every heartbeat, a spark ignites,
In the amber dusk, our soul ignites.

Underneath the Quiet Heat

Embers glow with tender grace,
In silence, we find our sacred space.
The warmth of you, a soft embrace,
In stillness, love takes its place.

Hands entwined, no need for words,
Our song is heard beyond the birds.
Through gentle sighs, our spirits soar,
Underneath the quiet, we seek for more.

Warmth in the Chilly Night

Snowflakes kiss the whispered air,
A blanket wrapped, a cozy share.
In frosted breath, our laughter plays,
Warmth ignites in wintry days.

The crackling fire, a dancing glow,
With every spark, our feelings grow.
In chilly realms, our hearts ignite,
Together strong, against the night.

Light Through the Veil of Solitude

In shadows cast, a light breaks through,
A gentle whisper, a vibrant hue.
Through solitude's grasp, we reach for grace,
Each moment shared, our sacred space.

Breathing life into the night,
With every gaze, you are my light.
Through veils of quiet, love defies,
In solitude's heart, our bond will rise.

Fireside Whispers

In the hush of night's embrace,
Flickering shadows dance and play.
Soft secrets in the glowing space,
Where fire's crackle holds sway.

Stories told with gentle grace,
Each spark a word, a fate entwined.
With every ember's subtle trace,
Memories linger, kind and blind.

The warmth seeps deep, a soothing balm,
Laughter echoes in the air.
Hearts alight, in the evening calm,
Bound by moments that we share.

Outside, the world may chill and freeze,
But here, the hearth keeps shadows at bay.
In tending flames, we find our ease,
In midnight stories, we find our way.

Warmth in the Silence

A blanket soft, the night unfolds,
Wrapped in whispers, still and clear.
With every heartbeat, warmth enfolds,
In silence, we find what's dear.

The stars above, in velvet skies,
Sparkle like dreams we dare to chase.
With quiet thoughts, our spirits rise,
In the stillness, we find our place.

The moonlight spills like silver lace,
Illuminating paths once lost.
Together, here, we weave our space,
In shared breaths, we pay the cost.

In shadows deep, we learn to trust,
The bonds of silence, strong and true.
In warmth we find, as all things must,
A refuge made from me and you.

Tapestry of Rays

Golden threads through skies of blue,
Kiss the earth with tender light.
In every hue, a vision new,
A dance of colors, bold and bright.

The morning dawns with whispered cheer,
As sunlight paints the waking day.
In gentle strokes, it draws us near,
To see the world in a brighter way.

Shadows fade with warmth's embrace,
Each moment weaving dreams so grand.
Together we shall find our place,
In this tapestry, hand in hand.

With every ray, our spirits soar,
Creating stories in the bright.
In love and joy, we ask for more,
A canvas rich with pure delight.

Bonds that Burn

In the heart of every flame,
Lives a dance that pulls us near.
Through heat and passion, strong the same,
Bonds that burn, forever dear.

Every spark ignites a wish,
Every flicker tells a tale.
In the warmth, we find our bliss,
In the glow, we shall not fail.

Like a candle, bright and fair,
Our choices shape the paths we take.
In the fire, our hearts laid bare,
Together strong, we shall not break.

In the ashes, love will rise,
Renewed with every challenge met.
For bonds that burn, beneath the skies,
Are flames that never will forget.

Unfurling Connections

In whispers soft, the hearts align,
Threads of fate begin to twine.
With gentle smiles, we reach and share,
Each bond we form, beyond compare.

Through laughter's dance, our spirits rise,
With every glance, the soul replies.
In moments small, we find our place,
An open heart, a warm embrace.

The world expands, as we explore,
In trusting hands, we find much more.
From silent nights to sunlit days,
Our ties grow strong in countless ways.

As seasons shift and journeys flow,
Through ebbs and tides, together grow.
No distance vast can keep us apart,
For love's sweet thread binds every heart.

In the tapestry, we weave with grace,
Each story shared, a treasured space.
Unfurling paths that brightly glow,
Together we face what lies below.

The Glow of Companionship

In twilight's hush, we find our way,
With laughter light, we greet the day.
Two souls entwined, through thick and thin,
A spark ignites, together we win.

With every word, a warmth we share,
A symphony sung in the evening air.
Our dreams entwined, a guiding star,
No matter where, we'll journey far.

Through shadows long, we share our fears,
Our laughter echoes, the world endears.
In quiet moments, hands held tight,
We face the dark, embrace the light.

Each heartbeat sings, a rhythmic tune,
In each other's eyes, a brightening moon.
Through storms that rage and skies so bright,
Our friendship shines, a beacon of light.

Together we blossom, roots that bind,
In the garden of life, the rarest find.
With you beside, the world aglow,
In every moment, love's seeds we sow.

Harmony in the Dark

In shadows deep, where whispers dwell,
A silent dance, a secret spell.
With tender grace, we weave our fate,
In quiet nights, we celebrate.

Our dreams take flight, like stars above,
In every heart, a song of love.
Through tangled paths, hand in hand,
In darkest hours, together we stand.

With every sigh, a story told,
Through whispered breaths, our souls unfold.
In the stillness, where fears collide,
Your strength is where my hopes reside.

As night unfolds, a canvas wide,
We paint our fears, but won't divide.
In harmony found, we trust and part,
Bringing light to shadows, heart to heart.

Together we rise, through every storm,
In warm embrace, we keep each other warm.
With courage found in the silent squall,
We find our peace when darkness calls.

Lightwoven Journeys

With every step, a story starts,
Across the miles, through beating hearts.
We wander pathways, bright and bold,
In lightwoven threads, our tales unfold.

Through valleys low, and mountains high,
In laughter shared, we touch the sky.
Each twist and turn, a lesson learned,
With love as fuel, our spirits burned.

The road may twist, and shadows play,
Yet hand in hand, we find our way.
In sunlit fields and thunder's roar,
Together we dream, forevermore.

Through landscapes vast, our hopes ignite,
In every moment, pure delight.
With every sunrise, new adventures call,
United we stand, never to fall.

In twilight's glow, our journeys blend,
With every thread, our hearts extend.
Together woven, strong and true,
Lightwoven journeys, me and you.

The Fire of Familiarity

In quiet glances, sparks ignite,
The warmth that holds our hearts so tight.
Through whispered words, we share our fears,
Embers burn bright across the years.

In laughter's glow, the shadows fade,
Like silent vows that we both made.
With every touch, the world feels right,
We dance together in the night.

Through shifting tides and stormy skies,
Our bond remains, it never dies.
In every moment, love's sweet grace,
Familiar paths, our sacred space.

As seasons turn and time moves on,
The fire of us will never be gone.
In hearts entwined, forever we stay,
A radiant blaze that lights our way.

Lifelines in Shadows

In stillness deep, where silence breathes,
We find our strength in whispered deeds.
A thread of light through darkest night,
Together we stand, ready to fight.

Beneath the weight of hidden fears,
We carry each other, through all the years.
In tangled paths, we walk as one,
With lifelines forged, our battles won.

As shadows loom, we rise above,
In every struggle, we find our love.
Through quiet storms, we learn to lean,
Together we trace what can't be seen.

In every heartbeat, courage found,
Our souls are anchored, safe and sound.
In this dance, forever entwined,
In shadows cast, our light we find.

Intertwined Flames

Two hearts ablaze in passion's dance,
Each flicker draws a fiery chance.
In every glance, a story's told,
Intertwined flames, both fierce and bold.

Through tangled roots, our spirits soar,
A burning love, we can't ignore.
In whispered dreams, we share our fears,
Together we thrive through all the years.

With every touch, the warmth ignites,
A vivid glow that sparks the nights.
In loyal bonds, our souls align,
Our intertwined flames forever shine.

As seasons dance and moments flee,
Our love endures, we'll always be.
In every heartbeat, hope remains,
A testament to our intertwined flames.

The Brightness of Us

In morning light, where shadows fade,
A canvas painted, hearts displayed.
With every laugh, the colors blend,
In the brightness of us, we transcend.

Through stormy skies and gentle rains,
Our love's a stream that never wanes.
In shared adventures, dreams take flight,
Together we carve a path of light.

With open hearts, we face the day,
Side by side, come what may.
In every gaze, a spark divine,
Illuminating, the world is ours to shine.

Through dusk and dawn, our spirits soar,
In every heartbeat, wanting more.
In each embrace, the warmth is true,
In the brightness of us, we always renew.

Whispering Warmth

In the quiet of the night,
Softly glow the stars so bright,
Petals dance in gentle air,
Whispers linger, sweet and rare.

Fires crackle, shadows play,
Hearts embrace in warm array,
Timeless stories softly told,
In their warmth, we find our gold.

Through the whispers, dreams take flight,
Holding close the fading light,
In this hush, our spirits soar,
Together, evermore explore.

As the moon begins to rise,
Reflected warmth in loving eyes,
Every sigh a sacred trust,
In this peace, we are robust.

Nestled close, we softly sway,
Wrapped in night till break of day,
In the dark, our hearts ignite,
Whispering warmth, our pure delight.

A Tinge of Togetherness

Hand in hand, we stroll the lane,
Sun-kissed fields, a sweet refrain,
Laughter dances on the breeze,
Moments shared bring hearts at ease.

Side by side, in joy we bask,
Simple pleasures, no great task,
Every glance, a cherished glow,
In this dance, together flow.

Starlit nights, our dreams unfurl,
In each other, we find our world,
Threads of life entwined and spun,
A symphony for two as one.

Through the storms, we'll stand so tall,
In our embrace, we conquer all,
Each heartbeat, a gentle sigh,
With a tinge, our souls comply.

Sunrise brings a brand new day,
Together, come what may,
Every moment, hearts will sing,
In this tinge, forever cling.

Hearts in Unison

Like two rivers, we flow along,
In each heartbeat, we belong,
Melodies of trust resound,
In our core, love is profound.

Eyes that meet, a spark ignites,
Through every loss, through every fight,
In the silence, whispers bloom,
Hearts in unison find their room.

With every laugh, with every tear,
Together, we will persevere,
In the fabric of our days,
Woven tight in love's embrace.

Underneath the starry skies,
Hand in hand, we realize,
In our rhythm, life's embrace,
Steady beat, our sacred space.

When shadows fall and doubts arise,
Trust will always be our guise,
Hearts beat steady, strong, and true,
In unison, me and you.

Twilight Revelations

As the sun surrenders light,
Colors blend in wondrous sight,
Whispers of the night do call,
In twilight's hush, we feel it all.

Stars begin to pierce the veil,
Cool winds echo through the trail,
Memories linger in the air,
With each breath, we linger there.

Shadows dance on the soft, cool ground,
In this twilight, truth is found,
Every secret gently spills,
Awakening the heart that thrills.

In the stillness, dreams ignite,
Luminous, our souls take flight,
Every sigh, a soft confession,
In twilight, sweet succession.

As day fades to night's embrace,
In twilight's calm, we find our place,
Revelations soft and bright,
In this moment, pure delight.

Whispered Bonds

In the quiet night, we speak,
Soft words that linger near,
A bond that seams the dark,
Wrapped in love and cheer.

Gentle hearts entwined tight,
In the depths of our trust,
Every sigh a promise,
Turning whispers to dust.

Fingers brush like the breeze,
In moments so sublime,
We share our secret dreams,
In the fabric of time.

Eyes that meet like the dawn,
Illuminating the path,
With every glance a spark,
Filling shadows with laughs.

Through silent tides we roam,
In rhythm and in flow,
Whispered bonds will carry us,
Where love continues to grow.

Radiant Echoes

Stars above softly gleam,
Reflecting hopes and fears,
In their radiant embrace,
We chase away the tears.

Echoes of laughter ring,
Through the night's gentle air,
A melody of our joy,
Crafting moments we share.

Lights that dance on the shore,
With waves that kiss the sand,
Each pulse a heartbeat's tune,
In a faraway land.

We weave our dreams like threads,
In a tapestry bright,
Radiant echoes of us,
Shimmering through the night.

As dawn begins to break,
Soft colors paint the sky,
Our hearts, a symphony,
Together, you and I.

The Glow Between Us

In the stillness of dusk,
A glow begins to rise,
Illuminating shadows,
Reflecting in our eyes.

Every word a whisper,
Every glance a delight,
The warmth of your presence,
Makes everything feel right.

We dance in silent harmony,
A rhythm only we know,
In the glow between us,
Love's gentle afterglow.

With every tender moment,
Colors start to blend,
The glow that we create,
Will never fade nor end.

Together in this journey,
With hearts wide open, true,
The magic in the silence,
Is the glow between us two.

Flickering Threads

In twilight's gentle haze,
Flickering threads unite,
Tales of love and laughter,
Told under soft moonlight.

Every heartbeat echoes,
As rhythms intertwine,
Threads of joy and sorrow,
We stitch with love divine.

Moments like fragile leaves,
Caught in a golden breeze,
We gather all the pieces,
Sewing life with such ease.

Through storms and through sun,
These threads will never break,
We'll weave a path unbounded,
In every choice we make.

So let the fabric flow,
In colors rich and bold,
Flickering threads of us,
A tapestry of gold.

Flickers of Familiarity

In shadows, whispers greet the night,
Memories dance in soft moonlight.
Familiar paths we wander still,
Each step a spark, a gentle thrill.

Old laughter echoes through the trees,
Carried softly on the breeze.
We find ourselves in fleeting glances,
Reviving past, igniting chances.

With every heartbeat, time unfolds,
Stories shared, and secrets told.
Nostalgic flickers, bright yet shy,
Illuminate the questions why.

A tapestry of love and grace,
Each thread entwined in our embrace.
Through flickers, we shall always find,
The warmth of hearts forever aligned.

The Subtle Glow

In twilight hues, the day must end,
Yet gentle light begins to blend.
A subtle glow, so soft and warm,
Invites the night to weave its charm.

Stars awaken, twinkling bright,
A secret language in the night.
The world transforms, a tender grace,
Illuminated in a sacred space.

Beneath the veil of soft-lit skies,
Dreams emerge, and spirits rise.
In shadows deep, we'll find our way,
Guided by this soft display.

With every breath, we shed our fears,
The subtle glow, it calms our tears.
In quiet moments, peace will show,
A promise held in the subtle glow.

Radiant Embrace

Morning breaks with colors bold,
A radiant embrace, a sight to behold.
Sunlight pours, like liquid gold,
Awakening dreams, the day unfolds.

With arms wide open, we greet the morn,
Kissing shadows, a new day is born.
Warmed by the sun, we rise and soar,
In every heartbeat, we crave for more.

Each ray a promise, a love so true,
Binding our spirits, me and you.
In this embrace, we find our place,
A radiant dance, our souls interlace.

As daylight wanes, we'll hold it tight,
The radiant embrace that ends the night.
Together we'll dream, forever awake,
In love's embrace, our hearts shall quake.

Trails of Luminescence

In the quiet woods, soft lights arise,
Drawing paths beneath twilight skies.
Trails of luminescence, we pursue,
Each shimmer a story, bright and true.

Fireflies dance in rhythmic flight,
Guiding the wanderer through the night.
With every glow, there's hope in sight,
As whispers of magic ignite the night.

Through dreams we walk, hand in hand,
Following secrets the stars have planned.
In the trails that shimmer and sway,
We find our love in gentle display.

With every step, the world transforms,
Wrapped in light, our hearts are warm.
Trails of luminescence in the dark,
Together forever, we leave our mark.

Heartbeats in the Dark

In shadows deep, whispers stir,
Silent echoes, hearts confer.
Stars above, like dreams take flight,
Guiding souls through the night.

A pulse resounds, a hopeful beat,
In darkness, warmth we meet.
Fingers brush in hushed embrace,
Finding solace in this space.

The moon's glow paints the world anew,
With every heartbeat, love rings true.
In this stillness, fears dissolve,
As heartbeats in the dark evolve.

A dance of shadows, soft and slow,
In secret gardens, emotions grow.
Each thump a promise, every sigh,
A symphony beneath the sky.

Together we weave a tapestry,
Of dreams and hopes, just you and me.
In the hush, our spirits sing,
In heartbeats dark, we find our spring.

Ties of Warmth

In winter's chill, two hearts entwine,
Sharing whispers, soft like wine.
Through frosted panes, our laughter glows,
A warmth that only true love knows.

With every touch, the cold retreats,
In cozy corners, love repeats.
Blankets wrapped, we share the heat,
Ties forged strong, our souls complete.

Candles flicker, shadows dance,
In this moment, we take a chance.
Eyes that shine like evening stars,
Our lives together, no more bars.

The world outside may freeze and fight,
In our embrace, it feels so right.
With every heartbeat, a vow we make,
In ties of warmth, our souls awake.

We dream of summers, love's bright glow,
But in this winter, feelings flow.
Our hearts, a fire, forever bound,
In ties of warmth, true love is found.

Threads of Light

Through twilight hours, the whispers weave,
Threads of light that we believe.
A tapestry of hope and dreams,
In every moment, that brightly gleams.

With every dawn, new colors burst,
In threads of light, we quench our thirst.
Stitched with laughter, joy, and grace,
Embracing life's warm, sweet embrace.

In gardens bloom, the flowers rise,
Patterns dancing under the skies.
A quilt of love, both fierce and strong,
In threads of light, we all belong.

Every spark ignites a hope anew,
Guiding us, as morning dew.
Across the fabric of endless night,
We find our way, through threads of light.

Together we weave this vibrant song,
In threads of light, where we belong.
Celebrating each stitch as it binds,
The essence of love that forever shines.

Silent Conversations

In glances shared, words unspoken,
Silent conversations, bonds unbroken.
A gesture here, a smile there,
In gentle moments, love lays bare.

With quiet hearts, we drift along,
In silent worlds, we both belong.
Each sigh a story, each breath a tune,
Under the gaze of a silver moon.

Time holds still, as spirits blend,
In fleeting glances, we comprehend.
With just a flicker, thoughts collide,
In silent conversations, hearts confide.

The language of love, a subtle art,
In silence, we speak, heart to heart.
Every heartbeat a gentle echo,
In this stillness, emotions flow.

As seasons change and moments pass,
We cherish the silence, that perfect glass.
In every quiet, we find our way,
In silent conversations, come what may.

Threads of Affection

In gentle whispers, hearts align,
Soft moments weaves a sacred line.
Within our laughter, secrets blend,
Each thread a bond, where love transcends.

Your touch, a spark, ignites the day,
Colors swirl in a warm array.
With every glance, we stitch and tie,
A tapestry beneath the sky.

Through seasons' change, our fabric grows,
Woven tales of highs and lows.
In stormy nights or sunny beams,
Threads of affection braid our dreams.

The distance shrinks when hearts are near,
In every heartbeat, I hold you dear.
A chorus sweet, our voices join,
In this vast world, you are my coin.

So let us walk on this path unknown,
With every step, our love has grown.
Together we'll weather the night and tide,
In these threads of affection, forever reside.

Light in Each Other's Eyes

In quiet moments, we find our way,
A spark ignites, no words to say.
Through soft gazes, deep truths unfold,
In the warmth of glances, love is told.

Every laugh shows a deeper light,
A flicker bright, softening the night.
In the silence, our hearts align,
A universe where love will shine.

With every tear, we share the load,
In this journey, hand in hand we go.
Your smile, a beacon in the dark,
Illuminates the spaces we embark.

We dance on dreams, in radiant hues,
Finding colors in the shades of blues.
Each sigh a promise, a tethered vow,
In the light of each other, we live now.

Through tempest trials, we rise and soar,
With a flicker that can't be ignored.
In the echoes of laughter and grace,
There's light in each other's eyes, a sacred place.

Signals of Connection

In the quiet hum of distant hearts,
A spark ignites, our journey starts.
Through subtle glances, a knowing glance,
The signals of connection weave romance.

With every heartbeat, a silent shout,
Undeniable ties, there's no doubt.
In shared smiles, the world feels whole,
The language of love, speaking to the soul.

In laughter's echo, we find our song,
A melody that carries us along.
With every whisper, we bridge the space,
Signal fires in this sacred place.

Through trials faced and joys we share,
In electric moments, love fills the air.
With every heartbeat, we rise and bend,
The signals of connection never end.

So let us dance in the cosmic flow,
Embrace the path where love will grow.
A tapestry of feelings that we explore,
In signals of connection, forevermore.

Illumination of Souls

In the quiet depths, our spirits shine,
Illumination, divinely aligned.
With every word, a candor glows,
In shared dreams, the essence flows.

Through the veil of night, we find our light,
Two souls converging, a beautiful sight.
With tender truths, we navigate,
Illumination opens every gate.

In the warmth of laughter, shadows fade,
In the glow of love, our fears are laid.
Each moment shared, a glimpse of grace,
The illumination of souls finds its place.

In storms, we gather, becoming one,
With every trial, new battles won.
Through time's embrace, our essence twirls,
Illuminated, we dance through worlds.

With every heartbeat, we learn and grow,
In the illumination, our spirits flow.
Together we shine, through darkest times,
In the illumination of souls, love climbs.

Illuminated Paths Intertwined

In shadows deep, we find our way,
Two souls aligned at end of day.
With whispered dreams, our hearts engage,
Each step we take, a turning page.

Beneath the stars, our fates entwine,
A dance of light, in rhythm divine.
The road ahead, both bright and clear,
Together forged, we have no fear.

As time unfolds, the night gives way,
To sunlit trails, where memories lay.
Through winding paths, our journeys blend,
Two hearts as one, forever penned.

Soft Radiance of Familiarity

In gentle beams, your laughter gleams,
A warm embrace, where love redeems.
The quiet moments, soft and pure,
In every glance, my heart's secure.

Like morning light on tender dew,
Your presence shines, a view anew.
With every sigh, a melody,
A comforting, sweet symphony.

Among the whispers of the night,
Your spirit glows, a guiding light.
Each shared breath, a sacred bond,
In soft radiance, we're both fond.

The Heat of Unspoken Words

Between us lies a silent spark,
A glance, a touch, ignites the dark.
In hidden depths, our feelings flow,
With every pause, a tale to grow.

The warmth of thoughts, not voiced aloud,
Creates a bond that feels so proud.
In sultry air, our spirits dance,
A secret world, where dreams advance.

The weight of silence, heavy yet bright,
Unveils the truths that hide from sight.
In whispered sighs, our hearts converge,
A gentle heat, where passions surge.

Glowing Signs of Interwoven Lives

In every moment, signs are shown,
The paths we tread, the lives we've known.
Through laughter shared and tears we shed,
Each glowing sign, by love is fed.

With every choice, our threads align,
In vibrant hues, our fates combine.
The echoes of our stories blend,
In every heart, we find a friend.

As seasons change, the ties grow strong,
A tapestry where we belong.
In woven dreams, the future thrives,
Together we shine, as interwoven lives.

Sparks of Solace

In the hush of night skies, we find,
Whispers of dreams that intertwine.
With every flicker, a story released,
Moments of peace, our souls are pleased.

Fleeting shadows dance in the air,
As laughter lights up, banishing care.
The warmth of a gaze, the spark of a grin,
Together we rise, let the night begin.

Fires may fade, but embers remain,
Carrying joy through both loss and gain.
In the silence, our hearts will mend,
Sparks of solace, love without end.

Time softly drifts, but we hold tight,
Binding our hopes in the cloak of night.
In each flicker, a promise we swear,
Forever in this moment we share.

With every heartache, we find our way,
In the warmth of each other, we choose to stay.
Through shadows and light, through laughter and tears,
In sparks of solace, we conquer our fears.

Glow of Kinship

In the meadow where sunlight gleams,
A shared bond dances, woven with dreams.
Together we wander, side by side,
In the glow of kinship, our hearts confide.

Branches may bend but never break,
Roots intertwined, in storms we wake.
With laughter and stories swirling around,
In the glow of kinship, love's magic found.

Stars above twinkle in delight,
As we recount our shared flight.
Through seasons of change, ever true,
In the glow of kinship, me and you.

Through trials faced, hand in hand,
Together we rise, together we stand.
A beacon of light when shadows ensue,
In the glow of kinship, forever renew.

Time cannot alter this radiant tie,
Through whispers of love, we learn to fly.
With every heartbeat, our bond ignites,
In the glow of kinship, we embrace the nights.

Interlaced Lights

In the tapestry woven with threads of gold,
Are stories of friendship waiting to be told.
Interlaced lights twinkle and shine,
A dance of our souls, forever align.

Every flicker reveals a new tale,
Of laughter and courage that will prevail.
Through valleys of shadows, through peaks so bright,
Interlaced lights guide us through the night.

In the silence shared, unspoken grace,
We find a rhythm, we find our place.
With every heartbeat, our spirits climb,
Interlaced lights, a love so sublime.

Bound by the moments we hold dear,
Together as one, we conquer our fear.
In the web of our lives, we've ignited the spark,
Interlaced lights, illuminating the dark.

As seasons pass and webs may shift,
In this journey together, we find our gift.
With each glowing strand, a bond so right,
Interlaced lights twinkle, spirits unite.

Heartstrings in Harmony

In the melody of life, we play,
Strumming heartstrings in a sweet array.
With notes that soar and whispers that fall,
In harmony, we answer the call.

A symphony of memories gently flows,
In laughter and tears, our love only grows.
In every chord, we find our grace,
Heartstrings in harmony, a warm embrace.

Through the highs and lows, we intertwine,
Creating a rhythm that's solely divine.
With every heartbeat, we stay true,
Heartstrings in harmony, just me and you.

When distance beckons, the music remains,
Binding us tighter through joys and pains.
No silence can dim the love that's bright,
Heartstrings in harmony, guiding our flight.

As the serenade of life carries on,
Our hearts keep singing, a timeless song.
Together we dance, our spirits ignite,
Heartstrings in harmony, love's pure light.

Flickers of Affection

In the quiet of the night,
Soft whispers take their flight.
A glance exchanged, hearts in sync,
Moments wrapped in loving ink.

Every touch a spark, a thrill,
Embers dance, a gentle will.
Breathless pauses, time stands still,
Together we climb each hill.

Gentle laughter rings so clear,
In our world, there's no fear.
With every heartbeat, bonds grow tight,
Flickers painting pure delight.

Like stars that twinkle far above,
Our souls weave tales of love.
Each secret shared, each sigh,
Flickers of affection never die.

The Light We Share

In shadows deep, we find our way,
With every step, we dare to play.
Two hearts alight under one sky,
Illuminated by love's high tie.

Hands entwined, we brave the night,
Chasing dreams, we chase the light.
Together we face the rising sun,
In this dance, we are as one.

Voices low, in harmony,
The light we share sets us free.
Each smile a beacon, bright and warm,
Through life's storms, we'll keep our form.

So let us shine, through thick and thin,
With every loss, there's still a win.
Together we'll face what lies ahead,
The light we share is love widespread.

Choreographed Radiance

In the ballroom of the night,
Every step feels just right.
With rhythm strong, we glide along,
Choreographed to our heart's song.

Twirls and spins, a dance divine,
In your eyes, the stars align.
Every glance, a move defined,
In this dance, our souls combined.

Soft whispers echo on the floor,
As we dance, we crave for more.
In each beat, a promise grows,
Choreographed in love's fine prose.

With every leap, with every sigh,
Together we soar, we touch the sky.
In the silence, our hearts proclaim,
Choreographed radiance, love's sweet name.

Flames of Affection

In the hearth where warmth resides,
Flames of affection, love abides.
With smoky trails that weave and dance,
In this fire, we find romance.

Each flicker tells a story true,
Of silent vows, just me and you.
With every spark, a memory's made,
Within this glow, our fears have frayed.

When storms may come to shake our ground,
In our flame, safety is found.
For through the dark, we brightly stand,
Flames of affection, hand in hand.

So let us stoke this fire bright,
Sharing warmth deep into the night.
Together we'll fuel this timeless spark,
Flames of affection lighting the dark.

Threads of Light Across the Void

In the quiet dark we roam,
Searching for a whispered home.
Stars above begin to gleam,
Weaving through each fleeting dream.

Paths entwined in cosmic grace,
Lifting hearts in soft embrace.
Fragments lost now found anew,
Guided by that brilliant hue.

Time and space begin to bend,
As we dare to seek and mend.
Threads of hope in shadows play,
Illuminating night and day.

With every pulse, the light expands,
Painting journeys with gentle hands.
Across the void, we chase the spark,
Finding warmth within the dark.

Together we ignite the fire,
Fulfilling every deep desire.
In this dance of light, we thrive,
Echoing how we come alive.

The Warmth of What Remains

Memories linger like soft songs,
Whispers of where the heart belongs.
In the silence, echoes bloom,
Filling spaces, lifting gloom.

Time has woven threads of gold,
Every touch a story told.
Through the years, the love we shared,
In gentle moments, hearts laid bare.

A photograph, a cherished glance,
Woven tight in life's vast dance.
The warmth of laughter fills the air,
Reminding us how much we care.

Though seasons change and shadows grow,
The light inside continues flow.
In the silence, hear the call,
Of those who've loved and lost it all.

What remains, a tender flame,
Flickering softly, ever same.
In each heartbeat, love's refrain,
Embracing all that will sustain.

Cascades of Radiance in Stillness

In the hush of dawn's embrace,
Gentle light begins to trace.
Cascades fall in golden streams,
Awakening our quiet dreams.

Nature whispers, soft and clear,
Bringing forth a sense of cheer.
Every petal, every leaf,
A symphony of sweet relief.

Moments pause in breathless air,
As beauty blooms beyond compare.
The stillness wraps us in its grace,
Radiating love in every space.

Lost in time, we find our way,
Guided through the break of day.
Cascades of light, a wondrous sight,
Filling our souls with pure delight.

In this calm, our spirits soar,
Reaching heights we can't ignore.
Together we will share the thrill,
Of radiance found in sweet still.

Sparked by the Breath of Memories

In the air, a whisper flows,
Carrying tales that love bestows.
Memories dance in twilight's haze,
Lighting paths through the maze.

Each heartbeat echoes, soft and clear,
Reminding us of those held dear.
Through the laughter, tears, and sighs,
A tapestry of life supplies.

Gentle winds, they bring us near,
To the visions we hold dear.
What once was lost now starts to rise,
Revealing all the hidden ties.

In the stillness, we shall find,
The breath of memories intertwined.
Sparked by love, a timeless glow,
Illumines paths where we must go.

With each step, our spirits bloom,
Filling every shadowed room.
Through the echoes of our past,
We find a love that's built to last.

Illuminated Souls

In the quiet glow of night,
Whispers dance in soft delight.
Hearts ablaze with vibrant light,
Guiding dreams to take their flight.

Through shadows deep, they weave their way,
Holding hands where spirits play.
Every laugh, a beacon bright,
Together they ignite the day.

In the chaos, calm and true,
Each soul shines, a different hue.
Connected by the silk of fate,
Emerging from what once was blue.

They shine like stars in darkened skies,
Gifted visions, clear and wise.
In every tear, a lesson learned,
Illuminated in their eyes.

With every step and every cheer,
Radiance grows, dispels the fear.
In each other, hope finds form,
Illuminated souls hold dear.

Bonds of Warmth

In the chill of winter's night,
Hearts entwined with pure delight.
Sharing stories, laughter flows,
With a touch that softly glows.

Through the storms that life may send,
Finding strength where friendships blend.
Hand in hand, we face the world,
In this warmth, our dreams unfurled.

Moments passed like gentle streams,
Filling life with tender dreams.
In the fold of kindred hearts,
Bonds of warmth that never parts.

With each hug a silent plea,
Know you'll always be with me.
In the tapestry we weave,
Countless memories that we believe.

As seasons change and time will race,
Love remains in every space.
Together through both dark and light,
Bonds of warmth will hold us tight.

Light in Darkened Corners

In the shadows, whispers call,
Flickers of hope that never fall.
Every heart a hidden spark,
Guiding those who roam the dark.

Through the maze of fears and doubt,
Shining truths begin to scout.
In the silence, strength is born,
Light in corners, hope reborn.

Together we will break the night,
Find our way, embrace the light.
In the cracks where darkness lies,
A million dreams begin to rise.

From the pain, we learn to fly,
With each tear, we touch the sky.
In the glow of guiding stars,
Light reveals our hidden scars.

With every dawn, a new embrace,
Shadows fade, we find our place.
In the warmth of love, we trust,
Light ignites what's pure and just.

Unspoken Harmonies

In a world where silence sings,
Unseen melodies take wing.
Harmony in every glance,
Connection blooms in subtle dance.

Underneath the moon's soft gaze,
Unspoken words weave golden rays.
Every heartbeat, a secret shared,
Invisible threads, always paired.

With each breath, a gentle tune,
Whispers rise beneath the moon.
Notes of kindness swell and swell,
In the stillness, all is well.

Through the chaos, find the space,
Where the heart can find its place.
In the pauses of the day,
Unspoken harmonies will stay.

Together we will compose a song,
In unity, where we belong.
With each note, a memory spun,
In the quiet, we become one.

Flickers of Affinity

In the hush of twilight's glow,
Two hearts beat soft and slow.
A rhythm found in silken air,
Whispers shared, a gentle dare.

Glimmers of trust, a bond is spun,
In laughter bright, two souls are one.
Like stars that weave the night above,
Every glance a thread of love.

Through landscapes wide, we wander free,
Mountains scaled, just you and me.
In every step, a promise made,
In every shadow, plans are laid.

In quiet moments, silence speaks,
A language known in shared peaks.
Together we'll chase the flowing stream,
Hand in hand through this shared dream.

Flickers chase the fading light,
Guiding us through the darkest night.
In each heartbeat, we're intertwined,
The flickers of affinity—divine.

Threads of Shared Light

Underneath the sweeping skies,
Two souls dance where the eagle flies.
With every thread of laughter sewn,
A tapestry of love is grown.

The softest hues of dawn's embrace,
In your smile, I find my place.
We wander paths of whispered dreams,
In sunlight's glow, light softly gleams.

Moments stitched with golden seams,
Binding hearts in woven dreams.
Through every challenge faced with grace,
We hold each other in this space.

The world may sway, the winds may change,
But the light between us won't rearrange.
With every giggle shared in cheer,
Threads tie us close, forever near.

In the depths of night's embrace,
We find our way with tender grace.
With each star, a wish ignites,
Threads of shared light spark the nights.

Glimmers of Togetherness

In the morning's tender light,
We find our paths, so clear, so bright.
With every step we take as one,
Glimmers shine as day's begun.

A laughter echoes, soft and warm,
Together we withstand the storm.
Through every trial, hand in hand,
We weave our dreams and take a stand.

The journey long, but hearts aligned,
In every moment, love defined.
We chase the sunsets, paint the skies,
Glimmers of hope in our eyes.

With stardust whispers, secrets shared,
In every glance, a love declared.
Through life's maze, we navigate,
United in a dance of fate.

In quiet night, when all is still,
Glimmers spark, our hearts fulfill.
With every sigh, our spirits rise,
Together, forever, under the skies.

Sparks in the Night

When twilight falls, our dreams ignite,
With laughter shared, we spark the night.
In whispered words, our secrets glow,
With each flicker, our spirits grow.

Beneath the stars, a canvas wide,
We paint our hopes with every stride.
In the dance of shadows, hand in hand,
Sparks of joy across the land.

Through winding paths and moonlit streams,
We chase the pulse of distant dreams.
With glances bright, we break the dark,
Together we share each vibrant spark.

In autumn's breeze or summer's heat,
Sparks fly where our hearts meet.
In laughter's ring and music's song,
We find our place, where we belong.

So let us roam through endless night,
With sparks alight, our hearts in flight.
In every moment, joy ignites,
Together, forever, sparks in the night.

Kindling Kindness

In the quiet of the night,
A spark ignites so bright,
With gentle words we share,
Fostering hope and care.

Each smile a glowing ember,
In hearts, kindness to remember,
With open arms we bind,
Creating warmth that's kind.

In the shadows of despair,
A tender touch laid bare,
As hands entwine with grace,
We find a sacred place.

The world can feel so cold,
Yet kindness makes us bold,
For every act, a flame,
In hearts we light the same.

Together we'll ignite,
A blaze that's pure delight,
With every shared embrace,
We kindle love's true face.

The Dance of Intimacy

In the stillness, hearts converge,
Like rivers at their urge,
Two souls in a tender sway,
A dance that words can't say.

With each glance, a story told,
In silence, warmth unfolds,
Entwined in softest light,
Every moment feels just right.

Fingers brush like autumn leaves,
In whispers, our heart weaves,
A rhythm deep and true,
In this dance, just me and you.

The world fades away from sight,
As shadows blend with night,
Our breaths synchronized,
In this space, we're realized.

Through time, let's move as one,
Underneath the setting sun,
In the warmth of our embrace,
We find our sacred place.

Together We Illuminate

In the dawn's early light,
We rise, hearts feeling bright,
Hand in hand, side by side,
In each other, we confide.

As shadows begin to play,
We push the dark away,
With laughter as our guide,
In love, we will abide.

Through storms and through the calm,
Together, we find our balm,
Lighting paths, shared and clear,
With every joy, we cheer.

In moments where we roam,
We build a shining home,
With every wish we make,
United, never break.

At sunset's glowing hue,
We'll share the test of true,
For in unity, we see,
Together, we're set free.

A Symphony of Glows

In the night, stars align,
A melody so fine,
With each twinkling light,
A symphony takes flight.

The moon plays a soft tune,
As shadows dance by noon,
In harmony, we sway,
Through night into the day.

Each heartbeat echoes clear,
As whispers draw us near,
In this vibrant embrace,
A rhythm we can trace.

As colors start to blend,
On this we can depend,
Together, hearts aglow,
In a sweet ebb and flow.

With every note we play,
Our spirits find their way,
In the music of our souls,
A symphony that consoles.

Dance of Glimmering Hearts

In twilight's glow, we take our chance,
With every step, we spark a dance.
Our hearts entwined, a vivid thread,
In rhythm sweet, where dreams are fed.

The moonlit sky, a silver hue,
Reflects the joy of me and you.
With every spin, the world fades away,
As stars above begin to sway.

Through gentle whispers, night unfolds,
A story of warmth, of love retold.
In every glance, a magic spark,
As we embrace the evening dark.

The music plays, our souls in flight,
Carried by winds of pure delight.
With every beat, our spirits soar,
Creating memories to adore.

When dawn arrives, and shadows part,
Forever etched within the heart.
This dance, this night, will never cease,
In glimmering light, we find our peace.

Illuminated Passages

In passageways made bright by dreams,
We tread where starlight gently gleams.
Each step reveals a hidden door,
To worlds where echoes long for more.

Whispers of time wrap us in care,
As memories linger soft and rare.
With every turn, the path unfolds,
A tapestry of stories told.

In corners where the shadows play,
We find the light that leads the way.
Together we explore the maze,
Guided by hope, through endless days.

With lanterns bright, our hearts ignite,
Illuminating darkest night.
Each moment shared, a starry spark,
In every hush, it leaves a mark.

As dawn ascends, the journey shifts,
Through illuminated, gentle gifts.
In treasured paths, our spirits roam,
In every heart, we find our home.

The Coals of Concord

In the hearth where embers glow,
We gather warmth, let feelings flow.
The coals of concord, bright and rare,
Bind us in love, a silent prayer.

With whispers low, we share our fears,
Each faded dream, through laughter, tears.
As stories rise, like smoke to sky,
In unity, we learn to fly.

Through trials faced, we stand as one,
In every struggle, we have won.
The flames of trust ignite the night,
Illuminating paths of light.

With every spark, new bonds take flight,
Creating warmth in dark's invite.
In harmony, our spirits dance,
A testament to love's sweet chance.

As daylight breaks, the coals still hum,
A symphony of where we're from.
In every heart, a story told,
Of concord's fire, forever bold.

Stolen Moments of Light

In fleeting hours of dawn's embrace,
We capture time, a cherished space.
With stolen moments, hearts collide,
Underneath the day's soft tide.

The world awakens, softly bright,
As shadows dance in morning's light.
Each breath we take, a gift divine,
In echoes sweet, our souls entwine.

With laughter shared, we paint the air,
In little joys, beyond compare.
Each fleeting glimpse, a treasure found,
In simple things, our loves abound.

Together we weave memories fair,
In secret places, time lays bare.
These stolen moments, pure and true,
Are threads of life that bind me to you.

When evening falls, and stars ignite,
We hold onto these beams of light.
In every heartbeat, love takes flight,
In stolen moments, hearts unite.

Dancing Shadows of Belonging

In twilight's glow, we sway and spin,
A symphony of whispers, where dreams begin.
Silhouettes entwined on the moonlit ground,
Each heartbeat a promise, in silence found.

Beneath the stars, our laughter glows,
Alive in the moment, where the river flows.
Every step echoes of stories untold,
In this dance of shadows, we break the mold.

With every turn, our fears dissolve,
In the warmth of belonging, our spirits evolve.
We twirl through the night, lost in the sound,
In the embrace of the dark, we are profound.

Together we weave, like threads in a seam,
Creating a tapestry birthed from a dream.
In this hallowed space, we are intertwined,
Dancing shadows, forever enshrined.

As dawn approaches, we'll share a glance,
A silent vow crowned in our dance.
With every flicker of light, we'll find,
In the twilight of belonging, our hearts aligned.

Radiant Echoes of Us

In the morning light, we rise anew,
Soft whispers of love, a vivid hue.
Every glance a promise, every touch a kiss,
In radiant echoes, we find our bliss.

Through bustling streets, hand in hand we roam,
Each heartbeat a reminder, this world is home.
In the laughter shared, in the tears we cast,
We build a future, leaving shadows of the past.

Moments like jewels, sparkling bright,
Together we shine, illuminating the night.
With every step forward, we carve our fate,
In the dance of existence, we celebrate.

As seasons change, our roots grow deep,
A garden of memories, in hearts we keep.
In vibrant colors, we flourish and thrive,
With each shared heartbeat, we feel alive.

Underneath the stars, our dreams will soar,
In the radiant echoes, we seek and explore.
Forever entwined, like morning and dew,
In this timeless melody, it's always us two.

The Hush Between Two Hearts

In the quiet moments, where silence sings,
Two hearts beat softly, wrapped in life's wings.
A gaze across the room, a secret share,
In the hush between us, love's tender care.

Gentle breaths like whispers, a calming tide,
Subtle connections we no longer hide.
In the pauses between, the universe sighs,
Where two souls collide beneath endless skies.

Every heartbeat echoes, a rhythm divine,
In the space that separates, we intertwine.
With fingertips grazing, the world fades away,
Anchored in this moment, forever we'll stay.

As twilight lingers at the edge of the night,
We find our solace in the soft, fading light.
In the hush between, all chaos departs,
Two souls in a symphony, where love imparts.

When words are no longer, and silence is loud,
In shared solitude, we stand unbowed.
For in that hush, a universe starts,
A world of devotion, between two hearts.

Flames of Shared Silence

In the hearth of quiet, embers glow bright,
Two souls huddle close, under soft starlight.
The language of silence, so deep and profound,
In flames of connection, our comfort is found.

With every shared glance, a story is spun,
In the warmth of the moment, we become one.
The night wraps around us, a velvet embrace,
In the flames of our silence, we find our place.

As sparks dance above, like thoughts in the air,
We breathe in the magic, two hearts laid bare.
With whispers of love, unspoken yet clear,
In the wilderness of night, we draw ever near.

Through shadows and light, our journey unfolds,
In the flames of shared silence, love's story is told.
A tapestry woven from trust and desire,
In the glow of together, we spark a fire.

With dawn on the horizon, the embers may fade,
But the warmth of our silence will never evade.
For in this connection, so profound and bright,
We kindle a flame that outlasts the night.

Glimmers of Togetherness

In the morning light we stand,
Hand in hand, soft and grand.
Whispers of joy fill the air,
Moments cherished, beyond compare.

Laughter dances, sweet and bright,
In the glow of shared delight.
Hearts entwined, a gentle thread,
Binding dreams yet to be spread.

Memories flicker, warm and true,
Woven paths of me and you.
Through the storms, we find our way,
Glimmers guide us day by day.

Together, we weather the night,
Stars align, our hopes in sight.
In the silence, love resounds,
In our unity, peace abounds.

Time may pass, but bonds remain,
In every joy, in every pain.
Glimmers of togetherness shine bright,
Forever our souls take flight.

Ashes of Yesterday's Laughter

Whispers fade like smoke in the breeze,
Echoes of joy bring me to my knees.
Memories linger, bittersweet sound,
In ashes of laughter, we're tightly bound.

The warmth of your smile, a distant dream,
Flickers like fire, a fading gleam.
Yet in the shadows, memories spark,
Illuminating paths through the dark.

Each tear that falls, a note in the song,
Reminding us where we both belong.
Even as time blurs the line,
Yesterday's laughter remains a sign.

From the embers rise moments so bright,
Remnants of love that once felt right.
In ashes of yesterday's embrace,
We find the strength to face each space.

Though laughter fades, it never dies,
In the heart's chambers, the spirit lies.
Cherish the echoes, let them fly,
In the ashes of laughter, we learn to cry.

Celestial Sparks Hidden Beneath

In the night sky, dreams take flight,
Whispers of stars, a shimmering light.
Beneath the surface, magic lies,
Celestial sparks in a world of sighs.

Each twinkle tells a story untold,
Woven in fabric, vibrant and bold.
We search for meaning in shadows cast,
In the hidden glow, shadows amassed.

Eyes closed tightly, feel the embrace,
Of cosmic wonders that time can't erase.
In silence, find the songs of the spheres,
Celestial rhythms that calm our fears.

With every heartbeat, the universe sighs,
Awakening dreams as the daylight dies.
Feel the connection, beyond the veil,
In the hidden beneath, our hearts prevail.

In the vastness, we find our place,
Dancing with stardust, lost in grace.
Celestial sparks, forever in reach,
Hidden treasures the night will teach.

In the Glow of Kindred Spirits

Together we gather, hearts in tune,
Under the silvery light of the moon.
In laughter and song, spirits ignite,
Binding us close, through day and night.

Kindred connections, woven tight,
In the warmth of friendship, everything feels right.
With every word, a gentle spark,
We find our way, lighting the dark.

Shared secrets and stories unfold,
In the glow of connection, we're never cold.
Each memory made a cherished jewel,
In the circle of life, we find the rule.

Across the miles, our spirits soar,
No boundaries can keep us from more.
In every laugh and every embrace,
We discover love in this sacred space.

In the glow, our hearts align,
Kindred spirits, forever divine.
Together we rise, together we dream,
In this beautiful dance, we're one team.

Flames of Understanding

In the quiet night, we spark,
Words like embers dance and glow,
With every story shared, a mark,
In the warmth, our hearts do know.

Through trials faced and joys combined,
We forge a bond that won't decay,
In each glance, a truth defined,
Our souls intertwined, come what may.

Fires may fade, but still we stand,
As shadows stretch and twilight falls,
Together, we can make a land,
Where silence speaks and love enthralls.

When storms arrive and doubts arise,
We'll hold the light, we won't lose sight,
With every laugh, every sigh,
Our flames burn brighter through the night.

So here's to us, to what we've built,
A tapestry of dreams so vast,
In the flames of understanding, felt,
Our story lives, forever cast.

In the Heat of Togetherness

Side by side, we face the day,
With laughter light and hearts so free,
In the heat, we find our way,
Together, just you and me.

The sun may blaze, the world may spin,
Yet here we stand, so strong, so rare,
In every loss, in every win,
We find our joy, we find our care.

Moments shared, each glance, each touch,
A warmth that we both can't deny,
In the chaos, you mean so much,
With you, my spirit learns to fly.

Let's dance in shadows, skip in light,
Join hands as we wander through,
In the heat of the day, so bright,
It's here with you, I feel brand new.

Through trial and strife, we stay as one,
In every heartbeat, trust remains,
In the heat, we've just begun,
Together, love breaks every chain.

Glow of Unseen Ties

In whispers soft, connections grow,
A thread we weave, both strong and fine,
Through quiet moments, love will show,
The glow that binds your heart to mine.

Invisible strands, they pull us near,
In every glance, in every sigh,
A bond so deep, so pure, so clear,
In the stillness, our spirits fly.

Through laughter shared and tears we hide,
The glow will guide us through the night,
No distance too far, no wave too wide,
As unseen ties pull tight and bright.

In secret places, truth takes flight,
Where only hearts can truly see,
Together, we emerge from night,
In the glow of our unity.

So let this bond forever shine,
Against the shadows, through all time,
With unseen ties that intertwine,
Our love, a radiant, endless rhyme.

Beneath the Surface

Beneath the waves, where silence dwells,
A world concealed from prying eyes,
In every heart, a story swells,
Mysteries wrap like whispered sighs.

We walk on paths that few can tread,
In every footprint, truth unfurls,
For in the dark, where dreams are bred,
We find the light that softly swirls.

What lies beneath is often rare,
The weight of love, the depth of pain,
Yet in the dark, we learn to care,
And from the shadows, hope we gain.

With gentle touch and knowing glance,
We'll dive into the depths unknown,
For in this dance, this fleeting chance,
Our souls unite, no longer alone.

So here we stand, submerged but bold,
In waters deep, our hearts immerse,
In mysteries wrapped, both warm and cold,
We find our truth, beneath the surface.

Flickers of Heartstrings

In the quiet night, stars play,
Soft whispers dance and sway,
Each flicker holds a name,
A spark ignites the same.

Flickers of Heartstrings

With every beat, the pulses weave,
Memories crafted, dreams believe,
In shadows cast by candlelight,
Our hearts align, a guiding sight.

Flickers of Heartstrings

Moments linger, time stands still,
A tender glance, an easy thrill,
Through all seasons, we will roam,
In every heart, we find a home.

Flickers of Heartstrings

A gentle touch, the breeze will share,
In laughter's echo, love declares,
These fragile threads, so deeply sown,
Together, we have always grown.

Flickers of Heartstrings

So let us dance beneath the moon,
Where every note is our sweet tune,
In harmony, we find our way,
Forevermore, come what may.

Flickers of Heartstrings

Through tangled paths, we journey forth,
In every sorrow, find the worth,
With heartstrings pulling ever tight,
We chase the dawn, embrace the light.

Whispered Flames of Affection

Beneath the sky, a soft caress,
Two souls entwined, a gentle press,
In the hush, our secrets bloom,
Like flowers bright within the gloom.

Whispered Flames of Affection

A flicker here, a glance from you,
In every shade, a vibrant hue,
The warmth we share, like summer's glow,
In the silence, love will flow.

Whispered Flames of Affection

With every laugh, the embers glow,
Through storms we weather, fast or slow,
In depths of night, we'll find the spark,
Embracing all, we leave a mark.

Whispered Flames of Affection

Two hearts aflame, a timeless dance,
In every chance, we find romance,
In whispered tones, we craft our fate,
Together strong, we celebrate.

Whispered Flames of Affection

So let the world fade to a blur,
In silent vows, our hearts confer,
With whispered flames, our journey's start,
Forever twined, two beating hearts.

Threads of Warmth in the Dark

In the stillness, shadows lay,
Threads of warmth guide our way,
With gentle hands, we weave and share,
Comfort found in utmost care.

Threads of Warmth in the Dark

In whispered tales that come alive,
Through every challenge, we survive,
A tapestry of laughter spun,
With every thread, our lives are one.

Threads of Warmth in the Dark

As seasons change and moments fade,
In love's embrace, we've always stayed,
A quiet strength, a bond so pure,
In darkest nights, love's light will cure.

Threads of Warmth in the Dark

Through winding paths, we find our way,
In every heart, we boldly stay,
Defying fate, we stand as one,
Two souls united, battles won.

Threads of Warmth in the Dark

With every breath, we share our dreams,
In whispered hopes, we find our themes,
So hold my hand, and hear my heart,
Together we'll write our own art.

Threads of Warmth in the Dark

In twilight's glow, our spirits soar,
With every heartbeat, we ask for more,
Ties that anchor, ties that free,
In love's embrace, we cease to be.

Unseen Ties that Bind

In silence shared, our hearts entwined,
Unseen ties that fate designed,
With whispered thoughts that go unsaid,
In quiet acts, our love is bred.

Unseen Ties that Bind

Through every storm, we find our way,
Like shadows dancing, night and day,
A strength so deep, it holds us fast,
In every moment, love will last.

Unseen Ties that Bind

In laughter's glow, in sorrow's tear,
These bonds we forge are crystal clear,
Through trials faced and joys embraced,
Love's quiet light cannot be replaced.

Unseen Ties that Bind

From distant shores, our souls connect,
With every gaze, we find respect,
In every heartbeat, rhythms blend,
Two paths converge, together mend.

Unseen Ties that Bind

Through stretches wide and mountains tall,
In gentle whispers, we hear the call,
The ties that bind, with strength so true,
In every heartbeat, I see you.

Unseen Ties that Bind

So take my hand, we'll face the night,
With every step, our hearts ignite,
In love's embrace, we find our ground,
In unseen ties, our truth is found.

9 781805 602712